Dahi Bhalla

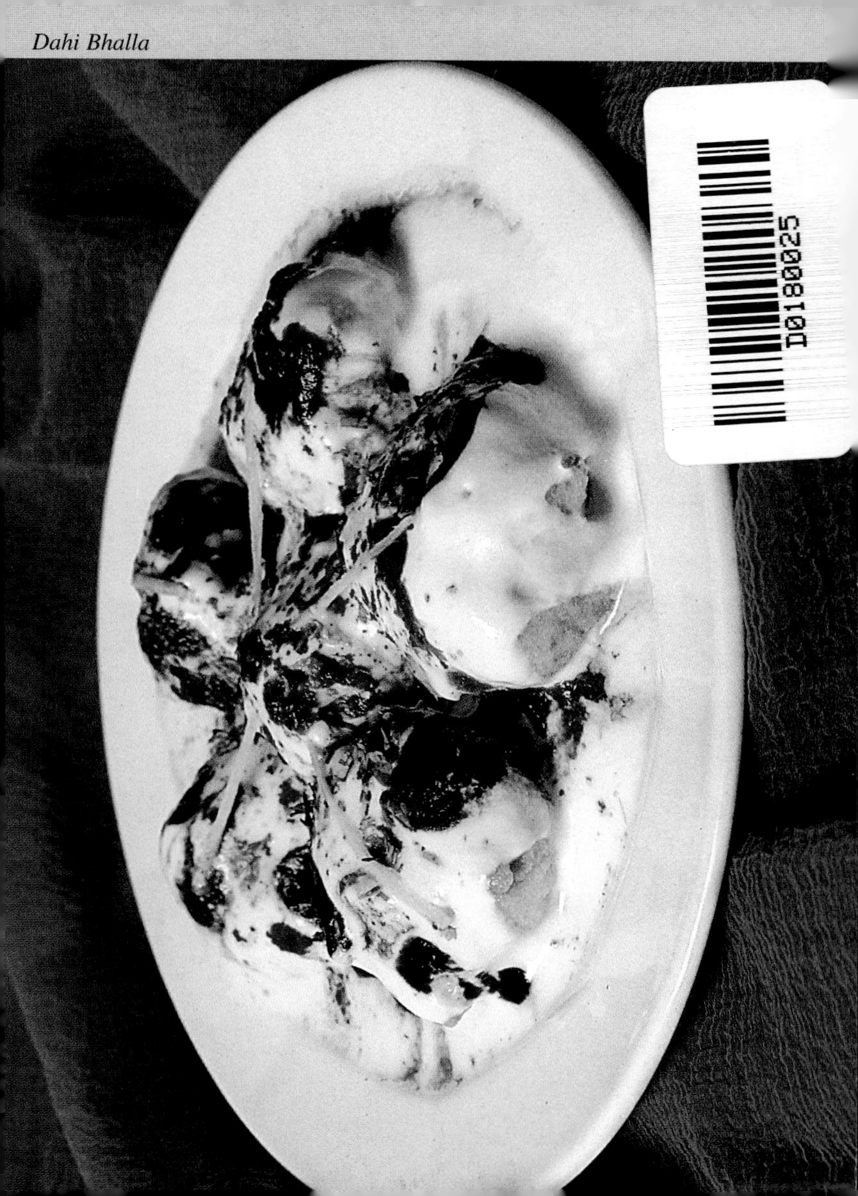

Kanchipuram Idlis

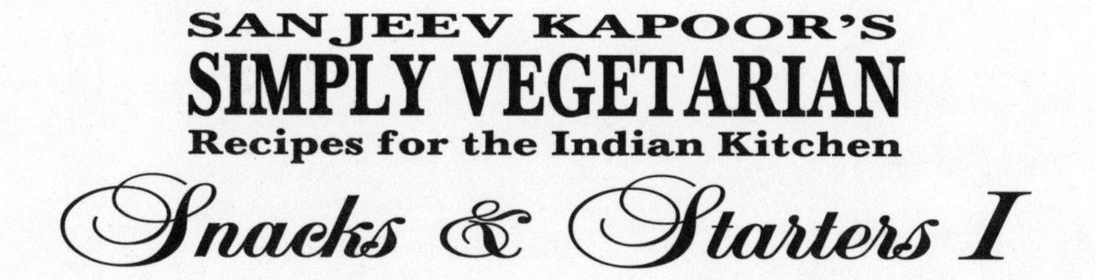
SANJEEV KAPOOR'S
SIMPLY VEGETARIAN
Recipes for the Indian Kitchen
Snacks & Starters I

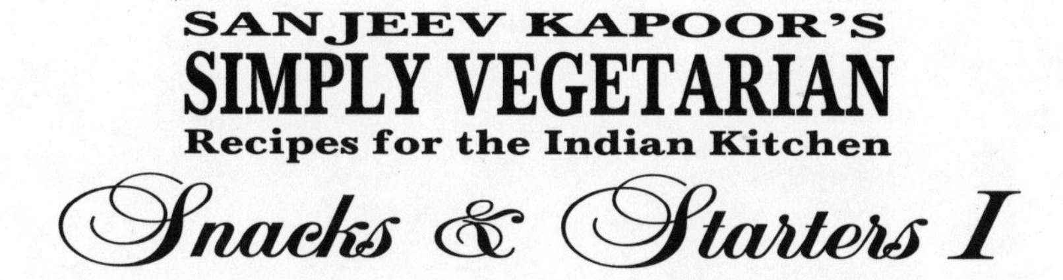

SANJEEV KAPOOR'S SIMPLY VEGETARIAN

Recipes for the Indian Kitchen

Snacks & Starters I

In association with Alyona Kapoor

POPULAR PRAKASHAN PVT. LTD.

First Published 2004

(3883)

ISBN - 81-7991-135-7

PRINTED IN INDIA
By Thomson Press (I) Ltd.
18/35 Milestone, Delhi Mathura Road, Faridabad (Haryana)
and Published by Ramdas Bhatkal
for Popular Prakashan Pvt. Ltd.

Exclusively Distributed by : Impulse Marketing

Dedication

To all the lovers of authentic
food whose enthusiasm makes us
dig deeper into the
Khazana of Khana, and come up
with what is best
and most precious in cuisine.

Acknowledgements

A.I. Kazi
Afsheen Panjwani
Anand Bhandiwad
Mrs. Lata Lohana & Capt. K. K. Lohana
Debashish Mukherjee
Dhiraj Bolur
Drs. Meena & Ram Prabhoo
Ganesh Pednekar
Harpal Singh Sokhi
Jijesh Gangadharan
Jyotsna & Mayur Dvivedi
Kishore Roy
Mallika Shetty
Manish Anand
Namita Pusalkar
Namrata & Sanjiv Bahl

Neelima Acharya
Neena Murdeshwar
Pallavi Sharma
Pooja & Rajeev Kapoor
Priti Surve
Rajeev Matta
Rutika Samtani
Sanjay Bakshi
Satish Parab
Shivani Ganesh
Smeeta Bhatkal
Swapna Shinde
Tripta Bhagattjee
Vinayak Gawande

Note to the Readers

What is a good snack? The one that has these two major ingredients: imagination and variety! Mealtimes are exciting, no doubt, but then there is many a palate that loves a snack or two to assuage the in-between hunger pangs. Snacks are also those delectable crunchies that one can serve friends who come visiting or dish up in a jiffy when unexpected guests drop in. Even though it is the age of the ready-made-just-open-the-packet goodies, many people are realizing that munching on potato wafers or indulging in confectioneries can take an adverse effect on one's health. I would say it is always better to have hygienic, well-prepared snacks at home that can add some health value to your daily intake.

Any good Indian snack will be made with precise specifications, skill and exact cooking time. The result is perfect, scrumptious, sometimes deep fried to a crisp, to be consumed on the spot and then some crispies can be stored in airtight containers to be relished later with friends. It cannot be denied that Indian snacks are becoming popular the world over and as the preparations are excellent in texture and flavour, the recipes are much wanted too.

If there is a favourite and versatile food then that is bread. It is a success as toast for breakfast, as a substitute for *rotis* at lunch, or as a sandwich with tea or as dinner rolls with soup for dinner! Adults and kids alike like my recipes of *Vegetable Hotdog, Brown Bread Sandwich* and *Apple and Cheese Toast*. We all enjoy having deep fried snacks like *samosas* and *kachoris* once in a while and something like *tikkis*, that can boast of a number of *avatars* are given here for you to try out. *Tikkis* can be made in the form of *Faldari cutlets*, or *Hariyali Tikki* or then the substantial *Moong Dal stuffed Aloo Tikki*.

If you are tired of having the same old things, it's time to try out the different *Black Grape Panipuri*, *Raj Kachori*, *Bread Bhelpuri* and what have you. They not only enliven the palate but also intrigue your friends who are bound to ask for the recipes!

In the same vein of adding variety we go global with *Burritos with Salsa Fresca*, *Sesame Corn Toast* and *Fried Herbed Mozzarella* to name just a few. Snacks can be healthy when made with healthful ingredients. And my philosophy is, once in a while, a deep-fried food cannot harm you. If at all one feels uneasy about indulging in fried snacks, I can only suggest they exercise regularly and seriously. Exercise alters the metabolism to such efficiency that one can eat without fear and especially those who love deep fried stuff must exercise as if the doctor's ordered it! The goldmine awaits your attention and lest one forgets, all recipes serve four and form part of a menu. So, go ahead and for once... indulge!

CONTENTS

Paneer Capsicum Pakora

Rawa Dosai

RAWA DOSAI

INGREDIENTS

Semolina (*rawa*) .... 2 cups
Rice flour .... 1 cup
Asafoetida .... ¼ tsp
Salt .... to taste
Ginger .... 1 inch piece
Green chillies 4
Dry coconut .... ¼
Cashewnuts 12
Peppercorns .... 2 tbsps
Cumin seeds .... 1 tsp
Pure *ghee* .... 2 tbsps
Oil .... to shallow fry

METHOD OF PREPARATION

1 Blend *rawa*, rice flour and two and one fourth cups of water to make a thin batter. Add asafoetida and salt.
2 Peel, wash and finely chop ginger. Remove stems, wash and finely chop green chillies. Grate dry coconut and crush cashewnuts. Add all these to the batter.

3 Crush peppercorns and cumin seeds. Heat *ghee* in a pan and fry peppercorns and cumin seeds lightly. Add to batter and stir well.
4 Lightly grease a non-stick *tawa*. Pour a ladle full of batter and spread by swirling the *tawa*.
5 Pour a tablespoon of oil around and on *dosa* and cook till it is crisp and golden in colour. Remove and serve hot.

CHEF'S TIP

The consistency of the batter should be pouring and not too thick. If you have spread the *dosa* thin enough then you need not cook the other side.

BLACK GRAPE PANI PURI

INGREDIENTS

Crisp *puris* 20-24
Fresh black grape juice .... 5 cups
Fresh mint leaves ..... ¼ small bunch
Fresh coriander leaves ... a few sprigs
Green chillies 3-4
Cumin seeds .... 1 tsp
Tamarind pulp .... 2 tbsps
Salt .... to taste
Black salt .... ½ tsp
Red chilli powder .... 1 tsp
Lemon juice .... 1 tbsp

For filling optional

Green gram (*moong*)
(sprouted) .... 1 cup

METHOD OF PREPARATION

1 Clean and wash mint leaves and coriander leaves. Remove stems and wash green chillies and grind them into a fine paste with mint and coriander leaves using sufficient quantity of water. Roast cumin seeds on a griddle and grind them into a powder.

2 Mix together fresh black grape juice, ground paste, tamarind pulp, salt, black salt, roasted cumin powder, red chilli powder and lemon juice.
3 Chill in refrigerator till use.
4 If you want to, you may fill each *puri* with a little sprouted green gram, then fill it up with grape juice mixture and relish this unusual *pani puri*.

NAMAKPARA

INGREDIENTS

Whole wheat flour (*atta*) .... ½ cup
Refined flour (*maida*) .... ½ cup
Baking powder .... ½ tsp
Ghee .... ½ cup
Salt .... to taste
Carom seeds (*ajwain*) .... ½ tsp

METHOD OF PREPARATION

1. Mix the two flours and baking powder. Add *ghee* and rub in with fingertips to get a consistency of breadcrumbs.
2. Add salt and crushed carom seeds. Add sufficient cold water to make stiff dough. Cover dough with a muslin cloth and let it rest for some time.
3. Sprinkle some refined flour on a flat surface and roll out dough into a half-centimeter thick diskette (*chapati*).
4. Preheat the oven to 200°C. Grease a baking tray with a little oil and sprinkle refined flour on it.
5. Cut rolled out dough into diamond shaped pieces. Place them on the baking tray and bake in the preheated oven at 200°C for fifteen to twenty minutes.
6. Serve hot or store them in an airtight container when cool.

CRACKLING SPINACH

INGREDIENTS

Spinach .... 2 medium bundles
Oil .... to deep fry
Sesame oil .... 2 tbsps
Red chilli flakes .... 1 tsp
Salt .... to taste
Sugar .... 1 tbsp
Sesame seeds (toasted) ..... 1 tbsp

METHOD OF PREPARATION

1. Wash, trim and drain spinach leaves. Pat dry thoroughly with an absorbent kitchen towel and cut into thin strips.
2. Heat sufficient oil in a wok, add spinach leaves and deep fry till crisp. Remove immediately and drain onto an absorbent paper.
3. Heat sesame oil in a wok, add red chilli flakes and immediately add fried spinach. Sprinkle salt, sugar and toasted sesame seeds.
4. Toss well to mix, remove into a serving bowl and serve immediately.

CHEF'S TIP

Since the water content in spinach is very high, add a little quantity of spinach first to stabilize the temperature of the oil before adding the remaining spinach.

CORNY POTATOES

INGREDIENTS

Potatoes .... 8 medium sized
Onions .... 2 medium sized
Garlic .... 6 cloves
Fresh coriander leaves ... a few sprigs
Celery .... 1 inch stalk
Butter .... 4 tbsps
Corn kernels .... ½ cup
Salt .... to taste
Pepper powder .... ½ tsp
Paprika powder .... ¼ tsp
Fresh cream .... ¼ cup
Cheese (grated) .... 2 tbsps

METHOD OF PREPARATION

1 Peel, wash and chop onions and garlic. Clean, wash and chop coriander leaves. Trim, wash and chop celery finely.
2 Wash potatoes with the skin and wrap in aluminium foil.
3 Preheat oven to 200° C. Bake potatoes for thirty to forty minutes or till done.
4 Remove a small bit of foil and potato skin from the top. Make a

hole in the potato by scooping out a bit from the center.

5 Heat butter. Add onions, garlic and celery. Sauté till onions turn golden brown. Add corn and sauté for three to four minutes.
6 Add salt, pepper powder and paprika powder.
7 Add coriander leaves and fresh cream. Stir well and allow it to cool.
8 Once it is lukewarm, put this mixture in the hollow potatoes and top it with grated cheese.
9 Bake in a preheated oven at 200° C till cheese is golden brown. Serve hot.

Corny Potatoes

Crackling Spinach

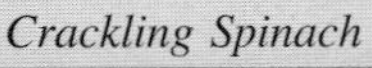

Burritos with Salsa Fresca

Vegetable Hotdog

VEGETABLE HOT DOG

INGREDIENTS

Hot dog buns 4
For rolls
Potatoes .... 2 large sized
Cottage cheese (*paneer*) ... 200 gms
Raisins 10-12
Fresh coriander leaves ... a few sprigs
Onion .... 1 medium sized
Green chillies 3-4
Red chillies whole 2
Oil .... 1 tbsp + to deep-fry
Garam masala powder .... 1 tsp
Refined flour (*maida*) ...... 4 tbsps
Salt .... to taste
Milk .... ½ cup
Bread crumbs .... 1 cup
To serve
Onions .... 2 medium sized
Green chillies 4
Lettuce .... 1 bunch
Butter .... 2 tbsps
English mustard paste .... 4 tsps
Tomato ketchup .... 4 tbsps

METHOD OF PREPARATION

1 Slit hot dog buns into half without cutting it into two.
2 Wash, boil, peel and mash potatoes. Grate *paneer*. Soak raisins in warm water for fifteen to twenty minutes. Drain and pat dry. Clean,

wash and chop coriander leaves. Peel, wash and chop onion. Remove stems, wash and chop green chillies. Remove stems, deseed and grind red chillies coarsely into flakes.

3 Heat one tablespoon of oil in a frying pan and sauté onion till translucent.
4 Mix together potatoes, *paneer*, raisins, red chilli flakes, sautéed onion, green chillies, coriander leaves, *garam masala* powder and salt. Let cool and divide into four portions.
5 Mix refined flour and salt together and keep it aside.
6 Shape potato mixture into cylindrical shaped croquettes. Roll croquettes in seasoned refined flour, dip in milk and roll in breadcrumbs. Keep them in the refrigerator for an hour or more.
7 Heat sufficient oil in a *kadai* and deep-fry croquettes till golden brown and drain onto an absorbent paper. Keep aside.
8 To serve, peel, wash and chop onions. Remove stems, wash and finely chop green chillies. Mix onions and green chillies. Wash, drain and shred lettuce.
9 Apply butter on the inside of the buns, apply mustard paste and place one spoonful of onion mixture. Spread tomato ketchup and arrange some shredded lettuce. Place a hot fried croquette, one in each bun and serve immediately.

BURRITOS WITH SALSA FRESCA

INGREDIENTS

Flour tortillas/flour *rotis* 4
Refried beans .... ½ cup
Onion .... 1 medium sized
Lettuce .... 1 small sized
Cheese (grated) .... ½ cup
Salsa Fresca .... ¼ cup

METHOD OF PREPARATION

1 Peel, wash and finely chop onion. Trim, wash, drain and shred lettuce leaves. Mix together beans, lettuce, onion and cheese.
2 Heat tortillas on a griddle plate *(tawa)* until hot and pliable but make sure they do not become dry.
3 Place two tablespoons of beans mixture a little below the center of the tortilla.
4 Top it up with Salsa Fresca and fold sides of tortilla over the filling to the center.
5 Fold bottom over filling and roll up, enclosing filling completely.
6 Serve immediately as burritos tend to become soggy very soon.

SALSA FRESCA

INGREDIENTS

Tomatoes .... 4 medium sized
Onion .... 1 medium sized
Jalapeno peppers 2
Lemon .... ½
Fresh coriander leaves ... a few sprigs
Olive oil .... 2 tsps
Vinegar .... 1 tsp
Salt .... to taste
Dry oregano .... 1/8 tsp

METHOD OF PREPARATION

1 Wash tomatoes and cut the base, making a cross slit on the topside. Immerse in boiling water for ten seconds. Remove and immediately put them in cold water.
2 Peel, deseed and chop them roughly.
3 Peel, wash onion and chop as finely as possible. Wash and finely chop jalapeno peppers.
4 Squeeze lemon, strain and keep juice aside. Clean, wash and chop coriander leaves finely.
5 In a medium sized bowl, combine tomatoes, onion and peppers.
6 Add olive oil, vinegar, lemon juice and salt. Crush oregano and add.
7 Mix well and let sauce stand for at least two hours to blend the flavours.
8 Serve at room temperature with your choice of snacks or as a dip for cocktails.

CHEF'S TIP

Red wine vinegar is recommended

DAHI BHALLA

INGREDIENTS

Black gram split (*dhuli urad dal*) ... . 1½ cups
Raisins 15-20
Salt .... to taste
Red chilli powder................ 1 tsp
Asafoetida....................... a pinch
Fresh coriander leaves..... a few sprigs
Ginger .... 1 inch piece
Green chillies 2
Oil .... to deep fry
Yogurt .... 6-7 cups
Rock salt (*kala namak*) .... 1 tsp
Mint chutney .... to taste
Tamarind chutney .... to taste
Roasted cumin powder ..... 2 tsps

METHOD OF PREPARATION

1 Wash and soak *dal* in three cups of cold water overnight. Drain off excess water the following day. Grind *dal* to a smooth paste. Wash raisins and pat them dry.
2 Whisk half a teaspoon of salt, half a teaspoon of red chilli powder,

raisins and asafoetida into the batter.

3 Clean, wash and chop coriander leaves. Peel, wash ginger and cut into julienne. Wash, remove stems and chop green chillies finely.
4 Heat sufficient oil in a *kadai*. Drop batter in tablespoonfuls in it and fry until light golden.
5 Remove, drain onto an absorbent paper. These are now called *bhallas* or *vadas*. Put *bhallas* in sufficient quantity of hot water. Leave for two minutes. Squeeze between your palms to drain out water.
6 Whisk yogurt well with rock salt (*kala namak*) and salt to taste.
7 To serve, place *bhallas* on a plate and cover with yogurt. Add mint *chutney* and tamarind *chutney*. Sprinkle red chilli powder and roasted cumin powder.
8 Garnish with coriander leaves, ginger julienne and chopped green chillies.

KANCHIPURAM IDLIS

INGREDIENTS

Rice .... 1 cup
Black gram split (*dhuli urad dal*) ..
.... ½ cup
Fenugreek seeds .... ¾ tsp
Turmeric powder .... 1 tsp
Peppercorns .... 2 tsps
Bengal gram split (*chana dal*) ... 2 tsps
Yogurt .... 1 cup
Asafoetida .... a pinch
Ghee .... ½ cup
Salt .... to taste
Tender banana leaves .... as required

METHOD OF PREPARATION

1 Wash and soak rice and black gram split with fenugreek seeds in three cups of water for three to four hours. Drain water and grind to a smooth paste.
2 Add turmeric powder, peppercorns, Bengal gram split, yogurt, asafoetida, *ghee* and salt. Mix well and let it stand overnight to ferment.
3 Whip batter and adjust consistency adding required quantity of water. It should be fairly thick.
4 Line *idli* cups with banana leaves and pour batter into them.
5 Steam for about twenty minutes or till done.
6 Serve with coconut *chutney* and *sambhar*.

PANEER CAPSICUM PAKORA

INGREDIENTS

Cottage cheese (*paneer*) ... 250 gms
Capsicums.......... 2 medium sized
Fresh coriander leaves .... 1 medium bunch
Fresh mint leaves .... 1 medium bunch
Green chillies 3-4
Lemon juice .... 1 tbsp
Salt .... to taste
Oil.............................. to deep fry

For the batter

Ginger .... ½ inch piece
Garlic ....2 cloves
Green chillies 2
Gram flour (*besan*) .... 1 cup
Cornstarch .... 3 tbsps
Baking powder .... ½ tsp
Turmeric powder .... ¼ tsp
Red chillies (crushed) .... 1 tsp
Salt .... to taste
Lemon juice ....1 tbsp
Oil ....1 tbsp

To serve

Chaat masala .... 2 tsps
Red chilli powder .... 1 tsp

METHOD OF PREPARATION

1 Cut *paneer* into one inch sized squares.
2 Wash, halve and deseed capsicums and cut into one inch sized squares.
3 Clean, wash and roughly chop coriander leaves and mint leaves. Remove stems, wash and roughly chop green chillies. Peel, wash and roughly chop ginger and garlic.
4 Grind together fresh coriander leaves, mint leaves, four green chillies to a fine paste. Add lemon juice and salt to taste. Separately grind together ginger, garlic and two green chillies to a fine paste for batter.
5 In a bowl mix *besan*, cornstarch, baking powder, turmeric powder, crushed red chillies, ginger-garlic-green chilli paste and salt. Add lemon juice and oil and mix. Add a little water to make a thick batter.
6 Spread green *chutney* on either side of the *paneer* squares. Stick capsicum squares on both sides of the *paneer* square.
7 Heat sufficient oil in a *kadai*.
8 Dip sandwiched *paneer* pieces in batter and deep fry till golden.
9 In a bowl mix *chaat masala* and red chilli powder.
10 Drain *pakoras* onto an absorbent paper. Cut into two halves. Place on a serving plate. Sprinkle dry *masala* and serve hot.

CORN PATTIES

INGREDIENTS

Corn kernels .... 1 cup
Fresh coriander leaves ....
.... ½ medium bunch
Green chillies 3-4
Ginger .... 2 one inch pieces
Cumin seeds .... 1 tsp
Bread .... 16 slices

Milk .... 1 cup
Coconut (scraped) .... ¾ cup
Lemon juice .... 1 tbsp
Sugar .... 1 tsp
Salt .... to taste
Oil .... to deep-fry

METHOD OF PREPARATION

1 Boil corn kernels in salted water for eight to ten minutes. Drain and keep aside.
2 Clean, wash and finely chop coriander leaves. Remove stems, wash and roughly chop green chillies. Peel, wash and roughly chop ginger. Grind green chillies and ginger to a coarse paste. Dry roast cumin seeds and crush lightly.

3 Cut bread slices into roundels using a cutter or a steel glass. Combine milk with half a cup of water and keep aside.
4 In a large bowl, combine corn kernels, scraped coconut, chopped coriander leaves, green chilli-ginger paste, cumin seeds, lemon juice, sugar, salt and mix well.
5 Dip two slices of bread in milk mixture, gently squeeze to remove excess water. Place a spoonful of corn mixture on one slice, cover with second slice and press gently to seal the edges. Similarly prepare the rest of the patties.
6 Heat sufficient oil in a *kadai* and deep fry the patties till golden and crisp. Drain onto an absorbent paper.
7 Serve hot with a *chutney* of your choice.

Note: The remaining edges of bread can be used to make breadcrumbs for later use.

VEGETABLE RAWA UPMA

INGREDIENTS

Semolina (*rawa*) .... 1½ cups
Carrot .... 1 medium sized
French beans 6-8
Cauliflower .... 1 medium sized
Capsicum .... 1 medium sized
Onion .... 1 medium sized
Ginger .... 1 inch piece
Green chillies 4
Green peas (shelled) .... ¼ cup
Curry leaves 10-12
Red chillies whole 4
Salt .... to taste
Oil .... 5 tbsps
Mustard seeds .... ½ tsp
Black gram split (*dhuli urad dal*) .... 2 tsps
Asafoetida .... ¼ tsp
Lemon juice .... 1 tbsp

METHOD OF PREPARATION

1 Roast semolina in a dry *kadai* without browning, remove and cool.
2 Peel, wash carrot and cut into small pieces. String French beans,

wash and chop finely. Wash cauliflower and break into small florets. Wash, halve, deseed and chop capsicum into small pieces. Peel, wash onion and ginger and chop finely. Remove stems, wash and finely chop green chillies. Wash and drain green peas. Wash and pat dry curry leaves. Remove stems and break red chillies into two.

3 Boil three cups of water, add a little salt and boil carrot, French beans, cauliflower and green peas for six to eight minutes or till the vegetables are almost done. Drain and reserve the vegetables.

4 Heat oil in a *kadai*. Add mustard seeds and as they begin to crackle add red chillies, *dhuli urad dal*, curry leaves and green chillies.

5 Mix well and add onion, ginger and capsicum and cook on high heat for two minutes. Add cooked vegetables, sprinkle asafoetida and salt to taste.

6 Pour four to five cups of hot water and bring to a boil. Add roasted semolina, stirring continuously to prevent lumps from forming.

7 Cook for three to four minutes on medium heat, stirring continuously. Stir in lemon juice and serve hot.

SENAI ROAST

INGREDIENTS

Yam .... 750 gms
Turmeric powder .... ½ tsp
Salt .... 1 tsp
Semolina *(rawa)* .... 1 cup
Oil .... to shallow-fry

For *masala*

Red chillies whole 8
Curry leaves 10-12
Cumin seeds .... 1 tsp
Fennel seeds *(saunf)* ...... 1 tbsp
Tamarind .... 1 lemon sized ball
Peppercorns (crushed) .... ½ tsp
Bengal gram split *(chana dal)* ... . 1 tbsp
Raw rice .... 1 tbsp
Salt .... to taste

METHOD OF PREPARATION

1 Peel and cut yam into fingers of approximately three inches x half inch x half inch. Wash well.
2 Boil yam fingers in four cups of water with turmeric powder and little salt till half-done. Drain. Cool and pat dry yam on an

absorbent towel.

3 To prepare *masala*, break off stems of red chillies. Wash and pat dry curry leaves. Dry roast all the *masala* ingredients on a *tawa*. Cool and grind to a smooth and thick paste.
4 Smear *masala* on the yam and refrigerate for about thirty minutes.
5 Roll yam in semolina and shake off the excess. Keep aside.
6 Heat oil in a shallow frying pan, and fry yam fingers in small batches. Roast on low heat till crisp and golden brown. Roll it continuously for even cooking.
7 Drain onto an absorbent kitchen paper and serve hot with your favorite dip.

CHEF'S TIP

Try this with potatoes or even sweet potatoes. Breadfruit *(Neer Fanas)* prepared in this method also tastes delicious.

BATATA CHIWDA

INGREDIENTS

Potatoes ....6-7 medium sized
Peanuts .... 1/3 cup
Cashewnuts .... 1/3 cup
Black raisins .... 2 tbsps
Red chillies whole 4
Sugar .... 2 tsps
Oil .... 2 tbsps + to deep fry
Cumin powder .... 2 tsps
Salt .... to taste

METHOD OF PREPARATION

1 Peel and wash potatoes, grate and keep them immersed in four cups of water.
2 Roast peanuts on a hot griddle and de-skin and similarly roast cashewnuts. Wash and pat dry black raisins. Remove stems and make small pieces of red chillies. Grind sugar to a powder and keep aside.
3 Heat two tablespoons of oil in a *kadai* and fry chilli pieces. Drain and keep aside. In the same oil fry raisins, drain and keep aside.
4 Drain water and pat dry grated potato by rolling it between folds of a dry cloth. Heat sufficient oil in a *kadai* and deep fry potatoes on low heat, till they become crisp. Drain onto an absorbent paper.
5 In a bowl mix fried potatoes, roasted peanuts, cashewnuts, black raisins, chillies, powdered sugar, cumin powder and salt.
6 Allow it to cool completely and serve or store in an airtight container.

Batata Chiwda

Raj Kachori

RAJ KACHORI

INGREDIENTS

Semolina (*rawa*) .... 1 cup
Refined flour (*maida*) .... 1 tbsp
Red chilli powder................ ¼ tsp
Salt .... to taste
Oil.............................. to deep fry

Filling

Potatoes .... 2 medium sized
Fresh coriander leaves ....
.... ½ medium sized bunch
M*oong* sprouts .... ½ cup
Chick peas (*kabuli chana*) ... ½ cup
Yogurt .... 1 cup
Maide ki papdi 10-12
Dahi bhalle 4
Cumin seeds .... 1 tsp
Rock salt powder .... ½ tsp
Red chilli powder .... 1 tsp
Tamarind *chutney* .... ½ cup
Green chilli *chutney* ...... 2 tbsps
Bhujia (*sev*) .... ½ cup

METHOD OF PREPARATION

1 Make stiff dough of *rawa*, *maida*, red chilli powder and salt with sufficient quantity of water. Divide into four to six equal parts, roll into *rotis* of around five inches diameter.

2 Heat oil in a *kadai* and deep-fry *rotis* in hot oil on medium heat, turning once, till well puffed and crisp. After they cool down, ensure that they are not soft. If they are, fry again. Keep aside. These are called *kachoris*.

3 Wash, boil, peel and cut potatoes into one centimetre sized cubes. Clean, wash and chop coriander leaves. Wash and drain moong sprouts. Soak *kabuli chana* in one and half cups of water for one hour. Boil it in a pressure cooker till two to three whistles. Whisk yogurt and dip *maide ki papdi* into it. Lightly mash *dahi bhallas*. Lightly roast cumin seeds on a griddle and make a fine powder.

4 Take one *kachori* in a serving plate. Make a big hole in the centre. Fill with potato cubes, sprouted *moong*, boiled *chana*, *papdi* along with yogurt and mashed *dahi bhalle*.

5 Sprinkle roasted cumin powder, rock salt powder, red chilli powder, tamarind *chutney*, green chilli *chutney*, *sev* and coriander leaves. Serve immediately before it becomes soggy.

FALDARI CUTLET

INGREDIENTS

Sweet potatoes .. 4 medium sized
Raw bananas...... 2 medium sized
Fresh mint leaves ....
.... ¼ medium bunch
Fresh coriander leaves ....
.... ¼ medium bunch
Ginger .... ½ inch piece
Green chillies 2
Raisins .... 2 tbsps
Cashewnuts 10
Almonds 10
Breadcrumbs (optional) ... ¼ cup
Oil .... to deep-fry

METHOD OF PREPARATION

1 Wash and boil sweet potatoes until soft. Cool thoroughly, peel and mash well.
2 Make slits on bananas and boil till soft. Cool, peel and mash.
3 Clean, wash and chop mint leaves and coriander leaves. Peel, wash and chop ginger. Remove stems, wash and chop green chillies. Wash, pat dry and chop raisins. Chop cashewnuts. Blanch almonds

in half a cup of boiling water for ten minutes. Drain, cool, peel and chop.

4 Combine mashed sweet potato and bananas with mint leaves, coriander leaves and ginger. Knead well to form a hard dough. If it is soft, add breadcrumbs.

5 Divide into twelve equal portions.

6 Mix raisins, cashewnuts and almonds and stuff this into each portion of above mixture. Shape each stuffed portion into a cutlet.

7 Heat sufficient oil in a *kadai* on moderate heat.

8 Deep fry cutlets in batches, turning over a couple of times, until golden brown and crisp. Drain onto an absorbent paper.

9 Serve hot with any sour *chutney*.

VEGETABLE KHASTA ROLL

INGREDIENTS

Potatoes .... 2 medium sized
French beans 7-8
Carrot .... 1 medium sized
Green peas (shelled) .... ¼ cup
Cauliflower .... ¼ medium sized
Fresh button mushrooms ....
.... 6 medium sized
Garlic .... 4 cloves
Green chillies 4
Fresh mint leaves ..... a few sprigs
Fresh coriander leaves ... a few sprigs
Tomatoes .... 2 medium sized
Onions .... 2 medium sized
Cucumbers .... 2 medium sized
Oil .... 1 tbsp + to deep-fry
Turmeric powder .... ½ tsp
Cumin powder .... 1 tsp
Salt .... to taste
Chaat masala .... 1 tsp
Cornstarch or refined flour (*maida*)
.... 1 cup
Yogurt .... 1 cup
Roomali rotis 4
Black salt .... ¼ tsp

METHOD OF PREPARATION

1 Wash, boil, peel and grate potatoes.
2 String, wash and finely chop French beans. Peel, wash and finely chop carrot. Wash and drain green peas. Wash cauliflower and break

into small florets. Place French beans, carrot, green peas and cauliflower in a colander and place on a pan of boiling water. Steam lightly for six to seven minutes. Drain well.

3 Clean, wash and quarter mushrooms. Peel, wash and chop garlic. Remove stems, wash and finely chop green chillies. Clean, wash and finely chop mint and coriander leaves.

4 Wash and chop tomatoes finely. Peel, wash and finely chop onions and cucumbers. Mix all these together and keep covered in a bowl. This is called *sambal*.

5 Heat one tablespoon of oil in a pan, add garlic and mushrooms and sauté for a minute. Add mixed boiled vegetables and sauté for two minutes.

6 Add turmeric powder, cumin powder and half of the green chillies, mint and coriander leaves and salt to taste. Mix and sauté for a minute.

7 Add potatoes and *chaat masala* and mix well. Remove from heat, transfer to a bowl and let cool. Divide into eight equal portions.

8 Shape into one and a half inch long finger-like rolls. Blend cornstarch in water to make a batter of thick consistency.

9 Heat sufficient oil in a *kadai*. Dip vegetable rolls in batter and deep fry till golden or alternatively, grill in a *tandoor*.

10 Mix together yogurt, remaining green chillies, coriander and mint leaves.

11 Place two vegetable rolls in a *roomali roti*, pour some yogurt mixture over. Sprinkle *sambal*, *chaat masala* and black salt. Roll up and serve immediately.

SABUDANA KHICHDI

INGREDIENTS

Sago (*sabudana*) .... 1½ cups
Peanuts .... ¼ cup
Green chillies 4-5
Potato .... 1 medium sized
Fresh coriander leaves ... a few sprigs
Curry leaves 7-8
Ghee .... 3 tbsps
Cumin seeds .... 1 tsp
Coconut (scraped) .... 2 tbsps
Salt .... to taste
Lemon juice .... 1 tsp

METHOD OF PREPARATION

1 Wash *sabudana* two to three times and soak in three cups of water for three to four hours. *Sabudana* grains should be separate and moist.
2 Roast peanuts on a hot griddle, remove skin and grind coarsely.
3 Remove stems, wash and finely chop green chillies. Peel, wash potato

and cut into half centimeter sized cubes. Clean, wash and finely chop coriander leaves. Wash and pat dry curry leaves.

4 Heat *ghee* in a pan, add curry leaves, cumin seeds and green chillies. When cumin seeds change colour add potato. Cook till potato is done.
5 Add *sabudana*, scraped coconut and ground peanuts, sauté for four to five minutes, stirring well.
6 Sprinkle a little water, add salt and lemon juice. Mix well. Remove from heat.
7 Sprinkle chopped coriander leaves and serve hot.

Sabudana Khichdi

Sev Batata Puri

SEV BATATA PURI

INGREDIENTS

Puris 24
Potatoes .... 2 medium sized
Raw mango .... 1 small sized
Onions .... 2 medium sized
Fresh coriander leaves ... a few sprigs
Salt .... to taste
Red chilli powder .... ¼ tsp
Coriander and mint *chutney* .....
.... as required
Garlic *chutney* .... as required
Tamarind *chutney* .... as required
Chaat masala .... as required
Fine *sev* .... as required

METHOD OF PREPARATION

1 Wash, boil, peel and dice potatoes into one-centimeter sized cubes. Peel, wash and finely chop raw mango into thin julienne. Peel, wash and finely chop onions. Clean wash and finely chop coriander leaves.
2 Arrange *puris* on a plate.
3 Mix potatoes, raw mango, salt and red chilli powder.
4 Place this over the *puris*.
5 Drizzle coriander and mint *chutney*, garlic *chutney* and tamarind *chutney* one on top of the other.
6 Sprinkle onions and *chaat masala*.
7 Cover up all the *puris* with plenty of *sev*. Garnish with coriander leaves and serve immediately.

RAJMA GALOUTI

INGREDIENTS

Red kidney beans (*rajma*) ..... 2 cups
Ginger .... 1 inch piece
Garlic .... 10 cloves
Green chillies 6
Fresh mint leaves ..... a few sprigs
Onions .... 2 medium sized
Cashewnuts 15
Sunflower seeds (*chironji*) ..... 2 tbsps
Poppy seeds (*khuskhus*) .... 1½ tbsps
Caraway seeds (*shahi jeera*) ... 1 tsp
Green cardamoms 8
Black cardamoms 6
Cloves 4
Cinnamon .... 2 inch stick
Saffron .... a generous pinch
Kewra water .... ½ tsp
Khoya/mawa (grated) .... 4 tbsps
Pure *ghee* .... 2 tbsps + to shallow fry
White pepper powder .... 1 tsp
Salt .... to taste
Lemon 1

METHOD OF PREPARATION

1 Pick, wash and soak *rajma* in five cups of water preferably overnight. Drain and boil in five cups of water until soft. Drain and keep aside.
2 Peel, wash and chop ginger and garlic. Remove stems, wash and finely chop green chillies. Clean, wash and chop mint leaves. Peel,

wash and cut onions into roundels.

3 Dry roast cashewnuts, *chironji* and *khus khus*. Grind to a fine paste using a little water.
4 Dry roast *shahi jeera*, green and black cardamoms, cloves and cinnamon. Grind to a fine powder. Soak saffron in *kewra* water.
5 Heat two tablespoons of *ghee* in a pan, add ginger and garlic and sauté for a few seconds. Add green chillies and sauté for one minute.
6 Add *rajma* and cook for three to four minutes.
7 Add cashewnut paste and stir-fry for four to five minutes.
8 Add *khoya*, white pepper powder and salt, stir-fry for four to five minutes.
9 Remove from heat. Cool and mash *rajma* to a smooth paste. (In case *rajma* paste is not firm, then cook paste further with addition of *ghee* till firm.)
10 Sprinkle powdered spices and soaked saffron. Adjust salt.
11 Add freshly squeezed juice of lemon and mix thoroughly. Divide mixture into equal balls and press them lightly.
12 Heat pure *ghee* in a frying pan and shallow fry *tikkis* until lightly coloured on both sides. Garnish with mint leaves and onion rings.
13 Serve with *chutney* of your choice.

PANEER TAASH KABAB

INGREDIENTS

Cottage cheese (*paneer*) ... 400 gms
Onions .... 2 medium sized
Tomatoes .... 2 medium sized
Mint *chutney* .... 8 tbsps
Cheese slices 8
Fresh cream .... 5-6 tbsps
Cheese (grated) .... 1 cup
Peppercorns .... ½ tsp

For marinade

Yogurt (hung) .... 1/3 cup
Red chilli powder .... 2 tsp
Coriander powder .... 1 tsp
Cumin powder .... 1 tsp
Ginger .... 1 inch piece
Garlic .... 4 cloves
Garam masala powder .... 1 tsp
Mustard oil .... 2 tbsps
Chaat masala .... to taste
Salt .... to taste

METHOD OF PREPARATION

1 Slice *paneer* into seven slices of two inches by two inches. Peel, wash and slice onion into roundels. Wash tomatoes and cut them into roundels. Roast peppercorns and crush them coarsely. Peel, wash and grind ginger and garlic to a fine paste.

2 Mix well all marinade ingredients and spread evenly on *paneer* slices. Keep aside for ten minutes.
3 Preheat oven to 150° C.
4 Spread mint chutney evenly on *paneer* slices.
5 Arrange onion and tomato roundels on each *paneer* slice and cover with cheese slice.
6 Stack each paneer slice with its layers one on top of other, by repeating the process.
7 Make a mixture of fresh cream, grated cheese and crushed peppercorns and pour over topmost layer.
8 Place last cheese slice on top and bake at 150° C for ten minutes
9 Cut into pieces of one inch by one inch. Serve hot.

CHUNKY MASALA POTATOES

INGREDIENTS

Potatoes .... 6 large sized
Olive oil .... 2 tbsps
Cumin seeds .... ½ tsp
Sea salt .... to taste
Peppercorns 6-8
Red chilli flakes .... 1 tsp
Lemon juice .... 1 tbsp

METHOD OF PREPARATION

1 Parboil potatoes for two minutes in five cups of water. Drain, cool and cut into thick wedges.
2 Preheat oven to 200° C. Grease a baking tray with half a tablespoon of olive oil. Lightly roast cumin seeds on a griddle.
3 Take sea salt, roasted cumin seeds, peppercorns and red chilli flakes in a mortar and crush coarsely with a pestle.
4 Take potato wedges in a bowl and sprinkle three-fourths of the crushed *masala* over them, add remaining olive oil and mix with a spoon.
5 Spread these potatoes on prepared tray evenly. Put in the preheated oven and bake at 200° C for fifteen minutes till done.
6 Sprinkle with remaining crushed *masala* and lemon juice and serve hot.

SAGO CHIWDA

INGREDIENTS

Sago (*sabudana*) .... 1 cup
Yogurt .... ½ cup
Salt .... to taste
Peanuts .... ¼ cup
Cashewnuts 20
Green chillies 4-5
Ghee .... to deep-fry
Sugar .... to taste

METHOD OF PREPARATION

1. Wash sago well and place in a colander so that it drains well.
2. Whisk yogurt with half a teaspoon of salt.
3. Mix sago and yogurt well. Keep aside for one to two hours.
4. Once softened, remove sago onto a piece of cloth and spread it to dry.
5. Dry roast peanuts and remove skin. Grind to a coarse powder.
6. Split cashewnuts. Remove stems, wash and chop green chillies.
7. Heat sufficient ghee in a *kadai* and fry sago a little at a time immersing it in a handled metal strainer. You might have to cover the strainer because sago splutters as it bloats up.
8. Drain fried sago and place it on an absorbent paper.

9 Once the sago is done, fry cashewnuts to a light golden colour. Drain onto an absorbent paper.

10 Fry green chillies till crisp.

11 Take a big bowl and mix all the fried ingredients with the peanut powder adding salt and sugar to taste.

12 When cool store in an airtight container.

HARIYALI TIKKI

INGREDIENTS

Potatoes .... 3-4 medium sized
Green peas (shelled) .... ¾ cup
Spinach *(palak)* .. 1 medium bunch
Green chillies 4-5
Fresh coriander leaves ... a few sprigs
Ginger .... 1 inch piece
Chaat masala .... 1 tsp
Salt .... to taste
Cornstarch .... 2 tbsps
Oil .... to deep-fry

METHOD OF PREPARATION

1 Wash, boil, peel and grate potatoes. Wash, boil and mash green peas. Wash, blanch spinach leaves in two cups of salted boiling water, remove and squeeze out excess water and finely chop. Remove stems, wash and roughly chop green chillies. Clean, wash and chop coriander leaves. Peel, wash and finely chop ginger.
2 Mix grated potatoes, peas and spinach. Add green chillies, coriander leaves, ginger, *chaat masala* and salt. Add cornstarch for binding and mix well to form a smooth mixture. Divide mixture into twenty-five equal portions.
3 Shape into balls and press each between the palms to give it a *tikki* shape.
4 Heat sufficient oil in a *kadai* and deep-fry *tikkis* until crisp. Remove and drain onto an absorbent paper and serve hot with a *chutney* of your choice.

BREAD BHEL PURI

INGREDIENTS

Bread slices 8
Oil .... to deep fry
Potatoes .... 2-3 small sized
Apple .... 1 medium sized
Lemon juice .... 1 tsp
Cucumber .... 1 small sized
Onion .... 1 large sized
Tomato .... 1 large sized
Fresh coriander leaves ....
.... ½ medium bunch
Peanuts (crushed) .... 1 tbsp
Sev .... ½ cup
Tamarind *chutney* .... ¼ cup

For tamarind *chutney* grind

Tamarind .... 1 cup
Jaggery (grated) .... 3 tbsps
Salt .... to taste
Black salt .... to taste
Cumin seeds .... ¼ tsp

METHOD OF PREPARATION

1 Take bread slices, trim off crust and cut into small squares (croutons).
2 Heat sufficient oil in a *kadai* and deep-fry bread pieces. Drain onto an absorbent paper and keep aside.

3 For tamarind *chutney*, soak tamarind in half a cup of water for fifteen minutes. Grind it along with remaining ingredients. Pass it through a sieve to get a smooth consistency.

4 Wash and boil potatoes. Cool, peel and cut into one centimeter sized pieces. Peel, wash and cut cucumber and apple into one centimeter sized pieces. Apply lemon juice to the apple pieces and keep aside. Peel, wash and chop onion finely. Wash and chop tomato finely. Clean, wash and chop coriander leaves finely. Crush peanuts and set aside.

5 Place bread croutons in a deep bowl. Add onion, tomato, cucumber, half of the coriander leaves, potatoes and apples. Mix well.

6 Add crushed peanuts, salt, tamarind *chutney* and mix well.

7 Sprinkle *sev* on top and garnish with remaining coriander leaves.

CORN DISC

INGREDIENTS

American corn .... 100 gms
Fresh bread slices 12
Butter .... 1 tbsp
Onion .... 1 medium sized
Garlic .... 5 cloves
Ginger .... ½ inch piece
Capsicum .... 1 medium sized
Tomato .... 1 medium sized
Fresh coriander leaves ... a few sprigs
Oil .... 2 tsps
Coriander powder .... ½ tsp
Turmeric powder .... ¼ tsp
Red chilli powder .... 1 tsp
Garam masala powder .... ¼ tsp
Salt .... to taste
Pepper powder .... to taste
Lemon juice .... 2 tsps
Cheese (grated) .... 2 tbsps
Onion seeds (*kalonji*) .... 1 tbsp

METHOD FOR PREPARATION

1 Wash American corn and keep aside
2 Cut bread slices into roundels using a cutter or a *katori*, apply butter and keep aside.

3 Peel, wash and chop onions finely. Peel, wash and grind ginger and garlic to a fine paste. Wash, deseed and chop capsicum and tomato finely. Clean, wash and finely chop coriander leaves.
4 Heat oil in a non-stick frying pan, add ginger-garlic paste and sauté for a minute. Add American corn along with onions, capsicum and tomato and cook for two to three minutes.
5 Add coriander powder, turmeric powder, red chilli powder, *garam masala* powder and stir-fry for two minutes. Add salt, pepper powder and lemon juice and allow it to cook for a minute. Remove from heat and allow to cool.
6 Preheat oven to 150°C.
7 Take a bread slice. Put one tablespoon of filling mixture, spread it evenly and top it with grated cheese and onion seeds.
8 Bake in the preheated oven (150°C) for five minutes or till cheese melts.
9 Serve hot with tomato ketchup.

PAPAD ROLLS

INGREDIENTS

Papads 8
Potatoes .... 4 medium sized
Green peas (shelled) .... ¼ cup
Ginger .... 1 inch piece
Fresh coriander leaves ....
.... 1 small bunch
Oil .... 1½ tbsps + to deep fry
Cumin seeds .... 1 tsp
Red chilli powder .... ½ tsp
Cumin powder .... 1 tsp
Turmeric powder .... ½ tsp
Chaat masala .... 1 tsp
Salt .... to taste
Gram flour *(besan)* .... 2 tbsps

METHOD OF PREPARATION

1 Wash and boil potatoes in sufficient water. Cool, peel and mash.
2 Wash and drain green peas. Parboil the peas in half a cup of salted water. Drain.
3 Wash, peel and finely chop ginger. Clean, wash and finely chop coriander leaves.
4 Heat one and a half tablespoons of oil in a pan and add cumin

seeds. When they change colour add ginger, parboiled green peas and stir-fry for a minute.

5 Add red chilli powder, cumin powder, turmeric powder, *chaat masala* and sauté for half a minute.

6 Add this to mashed potatoes along with salt and chopped coriander leaves and mix. Divide into eight equal portions. Make a paste of gram flour with one tablespoon of water.

7 Place one portion of the potato mixture on one side of a *papad* and spread evenly. Apply gram flour paste on the edges of the *papad* and roll. Fold the edges of the *papad* inwards taking care that the potato mixture does not come out.

8 Heat sufficient oil in a *kadai* and deep fry *papad* rolls for about a minute till crisp. Drain onto an absorbent paper and serve hot.

CHOLAFALLI

INGREDIENTS

Chavli flour .... 1½ cups
Salt .... to taste
Carom seeds (*ajwain*) (crushed) .... ½ tsp
Oil .... 2 tbsps + to deep fry
Red chilli powder .... ½ tsp
Chaat masala .... 1 tsp

METHOD OF PREPARATION

1 Mix *chavli* flour and salt. Add crushed *ajwain* and mix. Add one tablespoon oil and just enough water and knead into a stiff dough. Rest it for about ten minutes.
2 Pound the dough well, adding a little oil in between, till it is smooth.
3 Divide the dough into eight equal portions. Roll out each portion as thin as possible.
4 Heat sufficient oil in a *kadai*. Cut one-inch wide strips of the rolled out dough and deep fry till crisp. Drain onto an absorbent paper.
5 Mix red chilli powder and *chaat masala* powder and sprinkle over the fried strips when still hot.
6 Cool and store in an airtight tin. They will keep fresh for at least fifteen days.

Cholafalli

Papad Rolls

Bombay Pav Bhajee

Sesame Corn Toast

SESAME CORN TOAST

INGREDIENTS

Corn kernels (fresh) .... 1 cup
Sesame seeds (white) ...... 4 tbsps
White bread .... 4 slices
Capsicum .... 1 medium sized
Onion .... 1 small sized
Ginger .... 1 inch piece
Garlic .... 4-6 cloves
Green chillies 2-3
Fresh coriander leaves ... a few sprigs
Potatoes .... 3 medium sized
Soy sauce .... ½ tbsp
Cornstarch .... 3 tbsps
White pepper powder .... ½ tsp
Ajinomoto .... ¼ tsp
Salt .... to taste
Oil .... to deep-fry

METHOD OF PREPARATION

1 Clean, wash and finely mince corn kernels. Wash, halve, deseed and finely chop capsicum. Peel, wash and finely chop onion, ginger and garlic. Remove stems, wash, deseed and finely chop green chillies. Clean, wash and finely chop coriander leaves.

2 Wash, boil potatoes, cool and mash them in a bowl. Mix in minced corn.
3 Add onion, ginger, garlic, green chillies, coriander leaves, soy sauce, two tablespoons of cornstarch, white pepper powder, Ajinomoto and salt into the corn-potato mixture. Mix well. Blend remaining cornstarch with a little water to make a paste of medium thick consistency. Keep aside.
4 Cut bread slices with a cookie cutter to one and half-inch diameter discs.
5 Apply a thick layer of the corn mixture on the bread roundels. Apply a little of the blended cornstarch and dip into the sesame seeds. Shake off the excess seeds.
6 Heat sufficient oil in a wok and deep-fry prepared toasts for two to three minutes, stirring frequently or until crisp and golden brown in colour.
7 Remove, drain onto an absorbent kitchen towel and serve hot with assorted sauces.

BOMBAY PAV BHAJEE

INGREDIENTS

Potatoes .... 4 medium sized
Tomatoes .... 4 medium sized
Onions .... 2 medium sized
Green peas (shelled) .... ¼ cup
Cauliflower .... ¼ small sized
Green chillies 3-4
Fresh coriander leaves ....
.... ¼ medium bunch
Ginger .... 1 inch piece
Garlic .... 8-10 cloves
Capsicum........... 1 medium sized
Lemons 2
Salt .... to taste
Pav Bhajee Masala .... 1½ tbsps
Oil .... 3 tbsps
Butter .... 3 tbsps
Pav 8

METHOD OF PREPARATION

1 Wash, boil, cool, peel and grate potatoes. Wash and finely chop tomatoes. Peel, wash and finely chop onions. Wash and boil green peas in salted water till soft. Drain and mash lightly.

2 Break cauliflower into florets, wash and grate. Remove stems, wash and finely chop green chillies. Clean, wash and finely chop coriander leaves. Peel, wash ginger and garlic and grind to a fine paste. Wash, halve, deseed and finely chop capsicum. Wash and cut lemon into wedges.

3 Heat oil in a pan and add three-fourths of the onions. Sauté till light brown. Add green chillies and ginger-garlic paste. Stir-fry for half a minute.

4 Add half of the tomatoes and cook on medium heat for three to four minutes, stirring continuously or till oil separates from the *masala*.

5 Add capsicum, peas, cauliflower, potatoes and one and half cups of water. Bring to a boil and simmer for ten minutes, pressing with back of the spoon a few times, till all the vegetables are completely mashed.

6 Add *Pav Bhajee Masala*, salt and remaining tomatoes. Cook on medium heat for two minutes, stirring continuously.

7 Heat half of the butter in a thick-bottomed pan or on a *tawa*. Slice *pav* horizontally into two and pan fry in butter for half a minute, pressing two or three times or till *pav* is crisp and light brown.

8 Garnish the *bhajee* with chopped coriander leaves, remaining butter and serve hot with *pav* accompanied with remaining chopped onions and lemon wedges.

TURAI KABAB

INGREDIENTS

Ridge gourd (*turai*) .... 12 small sized
Cottage cheese (*paneer*) ... 500 gms
Onions .... 3 medium sized
Ginger .... 2 inch piece
Coriander seeds .... 2 tbsps
Green cardamoms 4
Peppercorns 12
Cinnamon ... 3 sticks of one inch
Ghee .... ½ cup
Cumin seeds .... 1 tsp
Yogurt .... 2 cups
Turmeric powder .... ½ tsp
Salt .... to taste

METHOD OF PREPARATION

1 Wash and slit ridge gourds and scoop out the seeds if they are mature. Crumble *paneer* and keep aside. Peel, wash and finely slice onions. Peel, wash and grind ginger into a fine paste.
2 Dry roast coriander seeds, cardamoms, peppercorns and cinnamon. Cool and powder.
3 To prepare stuffing, heat half of the *ghee* in a pan and add cumin

seeds and when they start to change colour, add onions and sauté till golden brown. Add one teaspoon of ginger paste and sauté. Add two tablespoons of water and continue to sauté.

4 Add a pinch of turmeric powder and powdered spices. Add *paneer* and salt and mix well. Sprinkle a few drops of water so that all the ingredients mix well.

5 Rub a little salt and one teaspoon of ginger paste on the inside of the slit ridge gourds.

6 Fill in stuffing into the slit gourds and tie with a thread.

7 Heat remaining *ghee* in another pan. Add stuffed gourds and cook on high heat till gourds turn reddish on all sides.

8 Lower heat. Add yogurt, remaining turmeric powder, salt, remaining ginger paste and mix lightly. Cover and cook on *dum* for about twelve to fifteen minutes.

9 Remove and serve hot.

BROWN BREAD SANDWICH

INGREDIENTS

Brown bread .... 8 slices
Butter .... 2 tbsps
Garlic .... 2 cloves
Shallots 5-6
Fresh button mushrooms 5-6
Celery .... 1 stalk
Cheese (grated) .... 4 tbsps
Olive oil .... 2 tsps
Paprika powder .... 1 tsp
Salt .... to taste
Pepper powder .... to taste

METHOD FOR THE PREPARATION

1 Take brown bread slices and apply butter on one side. Keep it aside.
2 Peel, wash and chop garlic. Peel, wash and chop shallots. Wash mushrooms under running water, pat dry and chop them finely. Trim, wash and finely chop celery.
3 In a non-stick frying pan, heat olive oil and saute garlic and shallots for two minutes.

4 Add mushrooms and celery and stir-fry for two minutes.
5 Add paprika powder, salt and pepper powder and saute for two to three minutes.
6 Remove from heat and use this as a filling.
7 Put half of the filling on one side of the bread slice and spread it evenly. Sprinkle grated cheese on top and cover it with a slice of buttered bread. Serve immediately.
8 Follow the same procedure for the remaining slices.

Brown Bread Sandwich

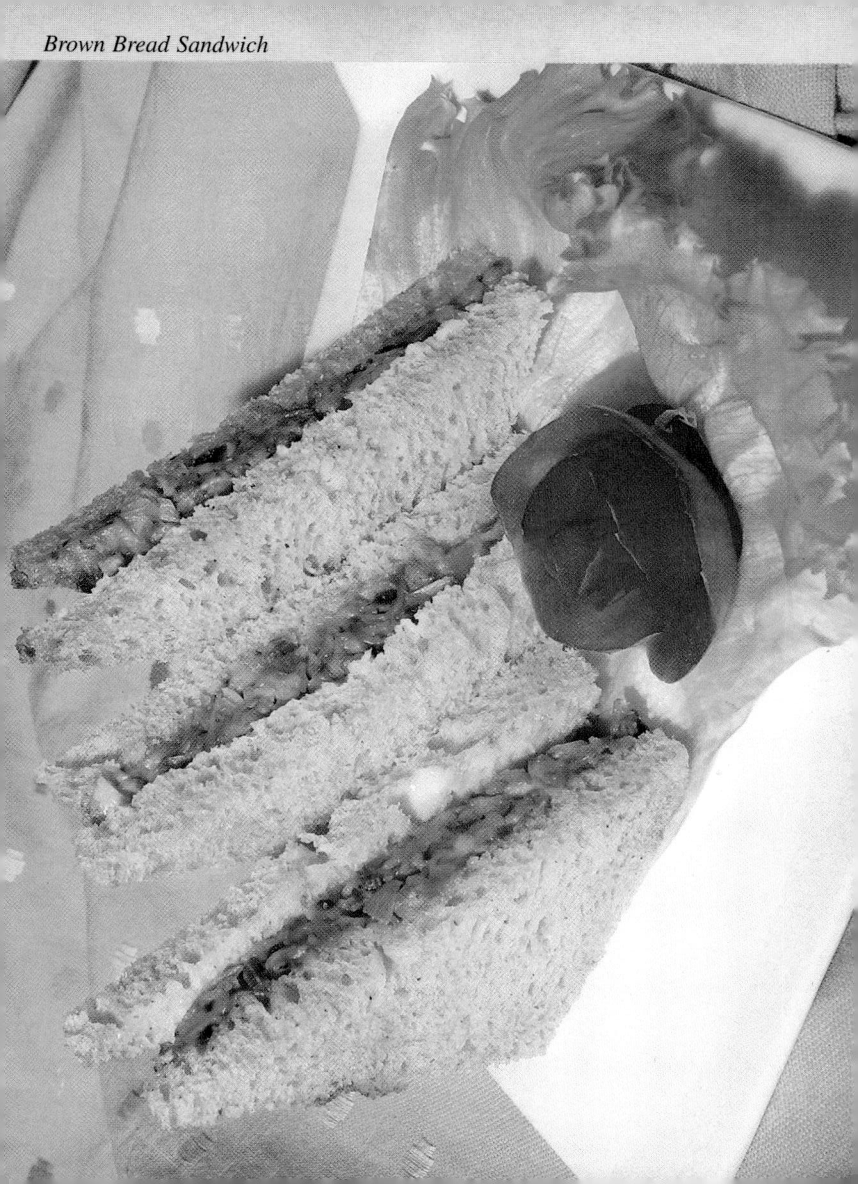

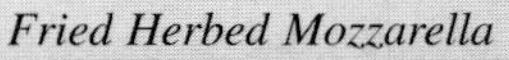

Fried Herbed Mozzarella

FRIED HERBED MOZZARELLA

INGREDIENTS

Mozzarella cheese .... 2 cups
Refined flour (*maida*) .... ¾ cup
Peppercorns .... ¼ tsp
Cornstarch .... ¼ cup
Salt .... to taste
Fresh parsley .... a few sprigs
Breadcrumbs .... 1 cup
Dried basil .... ¼ tsp
Oil .... to deep fry

METHOD OF PREPARATION

1 Cut mozzarella cheese into thick slices (one and a half inch square with one cm thickness). Sieve refined flour. Roast peppercorns and crush lightly. Clean, wash and chop parsley leaving a few leaves for garnish.
2 Mix refined flour, cornstarch, salt, crushed peppercorns and sufficient quantity of water in a bowl and mix to make a batter of coating consistency. Take breadcrumbs in a bowl. Add chopped parsley, dried basil and mix.
3 Dip mozzarella pieces in the batter and coat with breadcrumb mixture. Repeat this process once and shape with hand.
4 Heat sufficient oil in a wok and deep fry mozzarella slices till golden. Drain onto an absorbent paper. Cut into two and serve hot immediately garnished with a sprig of parsley.

LENTIL AND MINT PATTIES

INGREDIENTS

Red lentils split(*masoor dal*) ....1 ½ cups
Fresh mint leaves .... 1 medium bunch
Onions .... 2 medium sized
Garlic .... 3-4 cloves
Oil .... 3 tbsps + to deep fry
Tomato puree .... 2 tbsps
Dried breadcrumbs .... 1/3 cup
Salt .... to taste
Pepper powder .... to taste
Refined flour (*maida*) ...... 2 tbsps

METHOD OF PREPARATION

1 Pick, wash *dal* and soak in three cups of water for thirty minutes. Drain and leave aside.
2 Clean, wash and finely chop mint leaves. Peel, wash and chop onions and garlic.
3 Heat oil in a pan, add garlic, stir for a moment and add onions. Saute for three to four minutes till onions turn soft.

4 Add *dal* and cook for a three to four minutes.
5 Add about two and half cups of water and boil *dal* till soft and all liquid is absorbed.
6 Mash *dal*, cool and mix with tomato puree, mint, dried breadcrumbs, salt and pepper powder.
7 Divide it into small equal portions.
8 Form them into a round *tikki* shape and coat with refined flour.
9 Heat sufficient oil in a *kadai* and deep-fry *tikkis* until crisp and golden brown in colour. Drain onto an absorbent paper and serve hot with *chutney* of your choice.

PAUSHTIK POHA

INGREDIENTS

Pressed rice (*poha*) .... 2 cups
Soy granules .... ½ cup
Green chillies 3
Onions................ 2 medium sized
Fresh coriander leaves . ¼ small bunch
Curry leaves 8-10
Oil ....1 tbsp
Cumin seeds ....1 tsp
Roasted peanuts ....½ cup
Turmeric powder .... ½ tsp
Salt .... to taste
Lemon juice .... 2 tbsps

METHOD OF PREPARATION

1 Take *poha* in a colander, pour three to four cups of water evenly to moisten them. Drain well. Soak soy granules in one cup of water for fifteen to twenty minutes. Drain and keep aside.
2 Remove stems, wash and chop green chillies. Peel, wash and chop onions. Clean, wash and chop coriander leaves. Wash curry leaves and pat dry.
3 Heat oil in a non-stick pan and add cumin seeds. Stir-fry briefly. Add green chillies, curry leaves, turmeric powder and onions. Stir-fry for two minutes on medium heat. Add soy granules and sprinkle a quarter cup of water on it. Cook, covered, on low heat for five minutes. Stir well.
4 Add *poha* and toss over medium heat till it is heated through. Add roasted peanuts, salt and lemon juice. Toss well. Serve hot immediately garnished with chopped coriander leaves.

BHARWAN TIKKI

INGREDIENTS

For *aloo tikki*

Potatoes .... 3-4 large sized
Onion .... 1 large sized
Oil.. 2 tbsps
Cumin seeds .... ½ tsp
Salt .... to taste
Pepper powder .... 1 tsp
Fennel (*saunf*) powder ...... 2 tsps

For pea-spinach *tikki*

Potatoes .... 2 medium sized
Green peas (shelled) .... 1 cup
Spinach .... 7-8 leaves
Ginger .... 1 inch piece
Green chillies 3-4
Fresh coriander leaves ... a few sprigs
Oil .... 1 tbsp + to deep fry
Salt .... to taste
Cornstarch .... 3-4 tbsps

For corn filling

American corn .... ½ cup
Cheese (grated) .... ½ cup
Red chilli powder .... ½ tsp
Salt .... to taste

METHOD OF PREPARATION

1 Wash and boil potatoes for both *aloo-tikki* and pea-spinach *tikki*. Peel, mash separately and keep aside. Peel, wash and chop onion.

2 Wash, boil and mash peas. Wash spinach thoroughly under running water. Blanch them in two cups of boiling water for five minutes. Drain, refresh and chop. Peel, wash and chop ginger finely. Remove stems, wash and chop green chillies finely. Clean, wash and chop coriander leaves finely.
3 Heat oil in a pan. Add cumin seeds and when they change colour add onion and sauté for a half a minute.
4 In another pan heat oil and add chopped ginger.
5 Add mashed potatoes, salt, pepper powder, fennel powder to the first pan and sauté for a minute. Remove from heat. Transfer into a bowl.
6 To the second pan add mashed peas, chopped green chillies and sauté for a minute. Add chopped spinach and stir. Take care that the colour of spinach does not change. Add salt, mix and remove into a bowl. Add mashed potatoes, chopped coriander leaves and mix. Add cornstarch and mix properly.
7 Take equal portions of the potato mixture and shape them into balls. Put some oil on the tabletop, place the balls on them and

flatten slightly. Similarly prepare *tikkis* from the pea-spinach mixture. Use a cutter to cut both *tikkis* into roundels. With a smaller cutter cut a roundel from the center of the pea-spinach *tikki* to make it doughnut shaped. Now place the doughnut shaped pea-spinach *tikki* over the potato *tikki*.

8 Boil American corn and drain excess water. Add grated cheese, red chilli powder, salt and mix. Place a little portion of this mixture in the center cavity of the pea-spinach *tikki* and press lightly.

9 Heat sufficient oil in a pan and place *tikkis* in it. Gently agitate hot oil over the *tikkis* and fry till the potato portion turns golden. Drain onto an absorbent paper.

10 Serve hot with a *chutney* of your choice.

HARBHARACHYA PITHACHA KABAB

INGREDIENTS

Mayalu (*pui saag*) .... 1 medium bunch
Cinnamon .... 2 one inch sticks
Cloves 4
Green cardamoms 4
Peppercorns 10
Rice flour .... 1 cup
Salt .... to taste
Ginger .... 1 inch piece
Garlic .... 7-8 cloves
G*hee* .... to deep fry
Thick yogurt .... 1½ cups
Gram flour (*besan*) .... 1 tbsp
Turmeric powder .... ¼ tsp

METHOD OF PREPARATION

1 Clean and wash *mayalu* leaves in running water several times.
2 Grind cinnamon, cloves, green cardamoms and peppercorns into a fine powder. Add to rice powder. Add enough water to make a batter of coating consistency. Add salt to taste and mix.

3 Peel and wash garlic. Chop ginger and half the garlic cloves. Grind the remaining garlic cloves.
4 Heat sufficient *ghee* in a *kadai*. Dip *mayalu* leaves in the batter and deep fry till golden. Drain onto an absorbent paper. Reserve remaining batter.
5 Whisk yogurt with salt, gram flour and turmeric powder. Set aside.
6 In a pan heat some *ghee*, add chopped ginger and garlic and sauté till light brown. Add yogurt mixture and simmer. Add garlic paste and mix well. Add reserved batter and mix well.
7 Add fried *pakodas* and remove from heat. Allow standing time of few minutes for *pakodas* to absorb the yogurt. Serve hot.

VEGETABLE IDLI

INGREDIENTS

Parboiled rice *(ukda rice)* .. 1 cup
Black gram split *(dhuli urad dal)* .... ½ cup
Salt .... to taste
Carrot .... 1 medium sized
French beans 4-5
Cauliflower .... 2-3 florets
Capsicum .... ½ medium sized
Ginger .... 1 inch piece
Fresh coriander leaves ... a few sprigs
Oil .... 2 tbsps
Peppercorns (crushed) ...... 1 tbsp

METHOD OF PREPARATION

1. Wash and soak parboiled rice and *urad dal* separately for at least four hours. Drain and grind rice to a coarse and *dal* to a fine batter using enough water.
2. Mix both batters together, adding sufficient water to get dropping consistency.
3. Add salt and allow it to ferment for four to five hours or overnight, covered, in a warm place.

4 Peel, wash and grate carrot. String, wash and finely chop French beans. Wash and grate cauliflower florets. Wash, deseed and finely chop capsicum.
5 Peel, wash and grind ginger. Clean, wash and finely chop coriander leaves.
6 Add vegetables and ginger to fermented batter. Mix well.
7 Lightly grease *idli* moulds with oil. Pour a spoonful of batter into each mould. Garnish with crushed peppercorns and chopped coriander leaves.
8 Steam *idlis* till done. Allow standing time of five minutes, demould and serve hot with *chutney*.

SAUNFIA PANEER TIKKA

INGREDIENTS

Cottage cheese (*paneer*) ... 500 gms
Ginger .... ¾ inch piece
Garlic .... 5 cloves
Oil .... 2 tsps
Gram flour (*besan*) .... 2 tbsps
Turmeric powder .... ½ tsp
White pepper powder .... 1 tsp
Salt .... to taste
Lemon juice .... 1 tbsp
Green cardamom powder ... ½ tsp
Lucknowi fennel (*saunf*) powder
.... ½ tsp
Saffron (*kesar*) ...... a few strands
Fresh cream .... 1 cup
Butter .... for basting
Chaat masala .... 1½ tsps
Lemon juice .... 1 tbsp

METHOD OF PREPARATION

1 Wash and cut *paneer* into one and a half inch sized squares of half-inch thickness. Peel, wash and grind ginger and garlic.

2. Heat oil in a pan. Add *besan* and cook until it emits a fragrant aroma, remove from heat and add turmeric powder. Cool flour and transfer into a bowl.
3. Add ginger-garlic paste, white pepper powder, salt, lemon juice, green cardamom powder, fennel powder, saffron and fresh cream. Whisk well to make a batter.
4. Add *paneer* cubes to the batter and marinate for at least an hour.
5. Thread *paneer* cubes onto skewers two centimeters apart.
6. Roast in a *tandoor*/charcoal grill for five minutes, basting with melted butter occasionally till the *tikkas* are golden in colour.
7. Alternatively you can cook the *tikkas* in a convection oven or on a grill. Preheat the oven to 220°C and cook for three minutes on either side, basting once with butter in between.
8. Remove and sprinkle with *chaat masala* powder and lemon juice. Serve with *chutney* of your choice.

APPLE AND CHEESE TOAST

INGREDIENTS

Whole wheat bread .... 4 slices
Low-fat cottage cheese (grated) ... 1 cup
Apples .... 2 large sized
Lemon juice .... 1 tbsp
Cashewnuts 8
Orange juice .... ½ cup
Cinnamon powder .... ½ tsp
Honey .... 1 tbsp

METHOD OF PREPARATION

1 Wash, peel, core and cut apples into thick slices. Sprinkle lemon juice on apple slices.
2 Preheat oven to 175° C. Place cashewnuts in a baking tray and roast in the preheated oven till light golden. Alternatively, roast in a pan on medium heat. Cool and crush coarsely. Mix into the cottage cheese.
3 Heat a non-stick pan and gently poach apple slices in orange juice for about ten minutes or until just soft. Turn them over carefully for even cooking. Toast bread slices and trim off sides.
4 Spread cottage cheese mixture on the toasted bread slices and arrange cooked apple slices on top. Sprinkle cinnamon powder and place under a hot grill or in a preheated oven (180°C) until a light golden brown.
5 Drizzle honey on the hot toasts, cut into desired shapes and serve hot.

MOONG DAL STUFFED ALOO TIKKIS

INGREDIENTS

Potatoes .... 4 large sized
Salt .... to taste
Green gram split *(dhuli moong dal)*
.... 1 cup
Ginger .... 1 inch piece
Green chillies 3
Fresh coriander leaves ....
.... ½ small bunch
Turmeric powder .... ¼ tsp
Cumin seeds .... 2 tsps
Oil .... 1 tbsp + to shallow fry
Asafoetida .... a pinch
Lemon juice .... 1 tsp
Yogurt .... 1 cup
Rock salt .... ½ tsp
Red chilli powder .... ¼ tsp
Green *chutney* .... as required
Tamarind *chutney* .... as required

METHOD OF PREPARATION

1 Wash, boil, cool, peel and grate potatoes. Add salt and mix. Knead till smooth. Divide into small equal portions. Keep aside.
2 Wash *moong dal*. Drain.

3 Peel, wash and chop ginger. Remove stems, wash and chop green chillies. Clean, wash and chop coriander leaves.
4 Boil *moong dal* with salt and turmeric powder till just cooked (*al dente*).
5 Dry roast cumin seeds on a hot *tawa* till dark brown. Cool and grind to a fine powder
6 Heat one tablespoon of oil, add asafoetida, ginger, green chillies and parboiled *moong dal* and a little salt. Stir-fry for two to three minutes. Add lemon juice and spread on a plate to cool.
7 Add coriander leaves to *moong dal* and mix.
8 Take a portion of mashed potatoes in dampened palms, make a dent in the center, put some stuffing and close in the edges to enclose the stuffing. Press gently and roll the edges on the tabletop to smoothen the sides.
9 Heat a little oil on a *tawa* and shallow-fry *tikkis* on low heat till they turn crisp.
10 Whisk yogurt and add salt, rock salt, roasted cumin powder and red chilli powder.
11 To serve, place *tikkis* on a serving plate, pour some yogurt, green chutney and tamarind chutney over them.

Moong Dal Stuffed Aloo Tikkis

Apple and Cheese Toast